# 100 Best Strategies: Creating Innovative New Products

Richard Derks

ISBN-13: 978-1508515470
ISBN-10: 1508515476

# Contents

# Preface

This book is an action-oriented guide to strategies for developing innovative new products. The book is written in a checklist and workbook format. This format is a useful way to present a large number of such strategies in a concise manner, while encouraging the reader to immediately apply the content to their organizations. The strategic pointers should be viewed as seed matter for thinking—as notions to be fed and watered with rumination, while exposed to the light of the innovator's mind. Space is provided throughout the book for recording your own ideas and action steps immediately after reading each strategy. Rather than working through the book in one non-stop marathon session, I recommend you break it up into multiple sessions—either by chapter or so many strategies per session, or so much time per session. In this way, you will keep your energy level high while formulating your ideas and action plans.

The 100 pointers offered here are proven strategies discussed in many of the best books and articles on new product introduction. For many years, I have personally applied all of the lot—all 100—at one time or another, to projects over which I presided, and have proven to myself their value in the development of innovative products. There are, of course, other strategies being successfully applied in industry today that are not included in this book. This is not to suggest those strategies do not have value—but here I focus on what I and many others consider to be the most effective strategies currently in use.

For clarity's sake, examples are provided for some of the strategic pointers; examples are not provided when application of an idea is very straight-forward. A list of recommended books is also provided, for those readers who want to read more extensively on some of the strategies contained in this book.

Developing new products is almost always an exciting adventure, not without its (at least occasional) setbacks. I hope that the strategies outlined in this book minimize the setbacks and maximize the excitement. The acid test, however, will always be the financial success your products enjoy in the marketplace. I invite readers to share their experiences with me. And on the text itself, I welcome comments both critical and creative. You can reach me at: RichardPDerks@gmail.com

# Acknowledgments

Hundreds of people have contributed to this book in large and small ways. I am grateful to all the wonderful authors of books and articles who have documented their approach to product development. I also appreciate all the colleagues, professors, customers, and suppliers who have taught me so much over the years.

I am most appreciative to my wife, Sandy, who has supported me during all the years of college study, stressful professional work, and time dedicated to writing this book. I am also appreciative to my children, Alec and Stephanie, who had to put up with a dad who was much too often distracted by work obligations (and those never-ending emails) over the years. I want to thank my brother, Jeff, who applied his impeccable editing skills to ensure a smooth flow of text that makes sense in the end. And, finally, I give a special thanks to my parents who worked very hard throughout their lives and consequently taught me the value of hard work.

CHAPTER 1

# Introduction

Product Innovation. Everyone's talking about it. Annual reports always mention it, universities are striving for it, the government is begging for it, consultants are profiting from it, and it is hard to pick up a newspaper and not hear about it. But, is it really all that important? The answer is: yes!

According to a 2012 study by the consulting firm Cooper and Edgett, more than 30% of companies' revenues (across all industries) are generated by new products launched during the three years previous to the revenue appraisal. This percentage climbs to almost one-half—that's 50%—in electronic and computer industries. Also, there is a strong correlation between successful product innovation and business valuation. So it is little wonder that everyone's talking about product innovation: they should be.

For the purposes of this book, I shall define "innovation" to mean either a *completely new* product (or service) or *a significantly improved*, existing product (or service). This definition is consistent with most of the mainstream media, and with corporate usage. There is a small part of the academic community that uses a much more restrictive definition of innovation, to mean a completely radical new product that is disruptive in a marketplace. I prefer, however, to employ the more common usage of the term, with which most readers are familiar.

This book is meant to be a practical, hands-on source of strategies for helping companies accelerate their creation of new products. The one hundred strategies I have chosen to include are based on my experience as a product developer, the body of research on product innovations, and the many great books and articles on the topic of product innovation.

The strategies are organized into three main chapters: Creating the Right Environment—Involving the Right People—Following the Right Process. The checklist format makes this book quick to read, and easy to assimilate. Of course, its practical application is another, very much taller order. I recommend that you read through the book twice: the first time for understanding, and the second time for choosing those strategies you are most interested in implementing. Thereafter, retain it as a ready reference—a source of seeds for fresh thoughts, which the future will inevitably demand.

**CHAPTER 2**

# Creating the Right Environment

Developing innovative products starts with creating the right environment. You can have a great team and great processes, but if the physical and organizational environments are not conducive to product development, your chances for developing marketable new products will be sharply reduced. Creating the right environment means providing clear goals, sufficient resources, proper incentives, and the right physical accommodations.

**1. Eliminate obstacles to creativity.** Pull a cross-functional team together in your organization and make a list of all the factors about your organization that your team thinks impedes the creative process. This will likely include things like employees being overworked, fear of failure, jobs that contain too many high-pressure tasks, and so forth. For each of the obstacles your team identifies, brainstorm strategies for eliminating those blocks to creativity.

Ideas and Actions:

_____

_____

_____

_____

_____

_____

_____

**2. Publicize product successes within your company.** Employees are more motivated to push hard on new product development when they see the recognition that comes with bringing new products to market. Make every effort to publicize your new product successes. Leverage company newsletters, your intranet, your company web site, company meetings, annual reports, celebration lunches, and so forth.

Ideas and Actions:

_____

_____

_____

_____

_____

_____

_____

**3. Limit the number of new product development efforts.** Prioritize and allocate resources appropriately—taking into consideration payoff, risk, and resource requirements. This will keep your developers focused, working with high energy and creativity.

Ideas and Actions:

_____

_____

_____

_____

_____

_____

**4. Provide a feedback form on your web site; offer incentives for new product ideas.** Invite employees and customers to submit ideas; then publicize the successes. When customers and employees see that ideas are actually evaluated and sometimes implemented, they will be more likely to contribute.

Ideas and Actions:

_____

_____

_____

_____

_____

_____

**5. Believe in yourself and your vision.** Continuously remind yourself that hard work and a deliberate focus on innovation will pay off. Create a vision of taking successful new products to market and imagine all the great rewards (e.g., sales, bonuses, recognition) that can be reaped as a result of successful new products. Communicate this vision to your employees, to help them stay motivated and focused.

Ideas and Actions:

_____

_____

_____

_____

_____

_____

**6. Focus on excellence.** Demonstrate it and require it from your people. Set the bar high, letting your team know that you require excellence especially in the realm of new product development. You should personally embody this notion when participating in brainstorming sessions, vigorously generating ideas and encouraging others to do the same.

Ideas and Actions:

_____

_____

_____

_____

_____

_____

**7. Work on projects that you love.** Passion goes a long way in driving creativity and innovation. Allot at least 20% of your team's time for work on projects that team members truly value and enjoy. Just be sure the product development projects they choose fit with your company's strategy.

Ideas and Actions:

---

---

---

---

---

---

**8. Establish goals for new products in your organization.** Work with your team to identify the number of new product launches and sales/profit dollars you want to achieve from new products each year. Make the goals realistic, and then track your progress throughout the year.

Ideas and Actions:

---

---

---

---

---

---

**9. Remind yourself and your team of the value of failure.** The Wright Brothers and Thomas Edison were prime advocates of the philosophy that success is often bred of failure, which is why they never gave up when working on inventions. Emphasize to your team that failure is an opportunity to learn. Try to avoid penalizing anyone for failed products, focusing instead on "the moral of" the failure!

Ideas and Actions:

_____

_____

_____

_____

_____

_____

**10. Banish the myth of the non-creative type.** Everyone has the capacity to generate creative results. Unfortunately, many of us conclude early on that we are simply not a "creative personality," and we stop trying. Reject this notion, and push yourself to innovate. When you do come up with new ideas, take pride in this and use it as a reminder that you can be creative if you want to be.

Ideas and Actions:

_____

_____

_____

_____

_____

_____

**11. Change your routines.** Changing your daily, weekly, and monthly routine can be stimulating. In fact, diversify what you do in as many ways as you can. Drive to work a different way, have lunch with someone new, take up new hobbies, go to trade shows, read new magazines and newspapers. Diversifying what you do can refresh you and stimulate your creativity.

Ideas and Actions:

_____

_____

_____

_____

_____

_____


**12. Improve your work areas.** This can include introducing or changing the furniture, music, lighting, toys, or sports equipment. Get rid of anything in work areas that might interfere with your being creative (such as ringing phones and visitor traffic).

Ideas and Actions:

_____

_____

_____

_____

_____

_____

**13. Dedicate some work areas to ideation.** Spaces for idea generation should be separate and distinct from the usual day-to-day workspaces where your team performs their daily work. "Idea rooms" may contain flipcharts, Post-It's, a u-shaped arrangement of tables, private corners and carrels, and other furniture or equipment.

Ideas and Actions:

_____

_____

_____

_____

_____

_____

**14. Lower your public expectations of a project when appropriate.** Sometimes we make the mistake of establishing expectations that are too high—so high, that the product development team becomes mired in a fear of failure. A better strategy might be to downplay the role of the team to the rest of the organization, enabling the team to relax and relinquish fears of failure.

Ideas and Actions:

_____

_____

_____

_____

_____

_____

**15. Know and use the time, place, and situation when you are "at your best."** Some people are morning workers, some are better in the afternoon, and some are night owls. Some people work best in absolute quiet, while others like noise. Find what works best for you, then establish those conditions when you must perform creative work.

Ideas and Actions:

_____
_____
_____
_____
_____
_____
_____

**16. Work in places of preference.** Sometimes the best work is performed outside the regular office setting. This could be in a coffee shop, in the outdoors, or at home. Employ whichever setting seems best for creative insight on the task at hand.

Ideas and Actions:

_____
_____
_____
_____
_____
_____

**17. Ensure sufficient resources.** People work best at new products when they feel they have adequate resources and support. Ensure you provide adequate personnel, time, money, and equipment to support the development and launch of new products.

Ideas and Actions:

_____

_____

_____

_____

_____

_____

_____

CHAPTER 3

# Involving the Right People

Involving the right people can be one of the more challenging aspects of new product development. Hiring the right people to for new product development is far from a science, and often more fraught with trial-and-error than one would like. Fortunately, you can also draw upon suppliers, customers, distributors, consultants, independent inventors, and others to help compensate for any relatively weak employees you may have on your team. It is important to involve many different *types* of people in the development process so that, in the aggregate, you have enough talent to generate innovative products and bring them successfully to market.

**18. Use new employees, consultants, or professional facilitators for fresh insights.** New employees sometimes can bring new ideas and insights or will pose questions that stimulate creativity. Outside consultants bring the advantage of expertise, but can also contribute fresh perspective to your development efforts. Professional facilitators can bring out the best in your people and manage the team process for maximum results.

Ideas and Actions:

_____

_____

_____

_____

_____

_____

_____

**19. Leverage cross-functional teams.** Involving people from across your company will bring different perspectives and enhance the creative process. Be sure to involve Engineering, Marketing, Manufacturing, and Sales at a very minimum. Also, require all those who participate in new product development to periodically spend time in the field, interacting with your customers.

Ideas and Actions:

_____

_____

_____

_____

_____

_____

_____

## 20. Find people with multifaceted backgrounds.

The creative process is enhanced when participants have varied personal and professional backgrounds. Make sure your Human Resources Department works with you in achieving the ideal mix of diversity. Hiring outside your industry can be especially advantageous to enhancing creativity of the work team.

Ideas and Actions:

_____

_____

_____

_____

_____

_____

## 21. Rotate employees through different positions.

Encourage employees to learn all the dimensions of your business. Such knowledge will help foster both variety and quantity, in the generation of product development ideas.

Ideas and Actions:

_____

_____

_____

_____

_____

_____

**22. Cultivate a network of people from different industries and professions, with whom you can safely communicate your ideas.** Always select stimulating people for your network, as they will support you in your vision to launch innovative products.

Ideas and Actions:

_____

_____

_____

_____

_____

_____

**23. Generate product ideas with your suppliers and distributors.** Suppliers can often be a rich source of ideas since they know your industry, raw materials, technologies, and manufacturing processes. Distributors are often close to your product customers and may have a keen appreciation for customer likes and dislikes.

Ideas and Actions:

_____

_____

_____

_____

_____

_____

**24. Consider backward integration with suppliers, and/or forward integration with distributors.** Backward integration with suppliers can give you competitive advantages in raw materials and manufacturing processes. Forward integration with distributors can give you cost and delivery advantages, and move you closer to your end customers. For example, if you were a bicycle manufacturer, acquiring tire suppliers would be backward integration; acquiring stores that sell bicycles would be forward integration.

Ideas and Actions:

_____

_____

_____

_____

_____

_____

_____

**CHAPTER 4**

# Following the Right Process

Once you have recruited the right people and created the right environment, you have accomplished what many will say is the hardest part of creating new products. Nearly as difficult is adopting the right processes. There are many process strategies being followed by companies today, and many have been documented in the literature. This chapter outlines the best of the best, and provides examples for some of the more conceptually challenging ones. However, every company is unique, and there is no one right set of processes to follow. You should identify those strategies that fit your comfort level and produce the best results. Experiment, and find what works best for you.

**25. Follow good brainstorming rules.** In brainstorming sessions, strive for quantity, encourage wild or unusual ideas, elicit participation from everyone on the team, and forestall any criticism of ideas. Also, keep the pace moving, record ideas using the same terms participants use, and do not allow people to discuss ideas at length. Limit your brainstorming group to 5 to 12 people. Make the length of a single session at least 30 minutes, but no more than 60 minutes. Keep the pace moving. Do not criticize or compliment ideas as they are suggested. The atmosphere should be freewheeling.

Ideas and Actions:

_____

_____

_____

_____

_____

_____

**26. Combine apparently disparate ideas.** Sometimes, more creative solutions can result when you combine ideas on a list, even though they may not initially seem related.

Example: Automobile Design

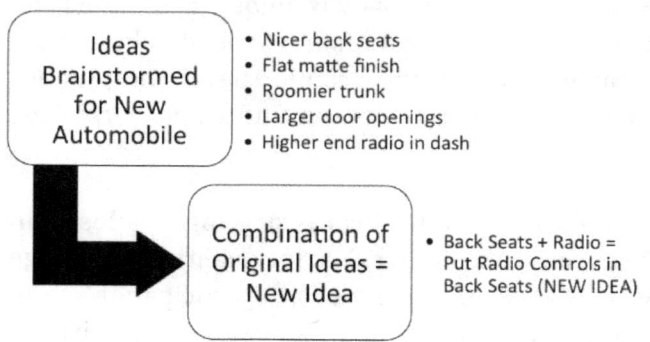

Ideas Brainstormed for New Automobile
- Nicer back seats
- Flat matte finish
- Roomier trunk
- Larger door openings
- Higher end radio in dash

Combination of Original Ideas = New Idea
- Back Seats + Radio = Put Radio Controls in Back Seats (NEW IDEA)

Ideas and Actions:

_____

_____

_____

_____

_____

_____

**27. Be vigilant for new ideas across time.**
Innovative ideas can surface anytime, and anywhere.
Devise a simple way to capture new ideas when they
arise. Use a notebook, a voice recorder, a
smartphone—whatever means is simplest and most
convenient.

Ideas and Actions:

_____

_____

_____

_____

_____

_____

**28. Maintain a "bug list."** Be alert, in daily life, for
small things that bother (or "bug") you. Daily routine
nuisances are easily taken for granted—but may well
be signals of products that need improving. Rather
than accepting or trying to resolve problems on the
spot, document them on a bug list, for later
brainstorming and resolution.

Ideas and Actions:

_____

_____

_____

_____

_____

_____

_____

**29. Focus on eco-friendliness.** Sustainability is increasingly important, not only from the standpoint of preserving resources and reducing costs of manufacture, but also for improving marketability of end products. Focusing on sustainability can generate a wealth of ideas for improving existing products.

Ideas and Actions:

_____

_____

_____

_____

_____

_____

_____

**30. Develop products that leverage hybrid energy sources.** Energy efficiency in manufacturing impacts marketability—especially as the market of eco-friendly consumers grows.

Ideas and Actions:

_____

_____

_____

_____

_____

_____

_____

**31. Brainstorm applications of new technology.** Keep yourself informed on new developments in science and technology, even those not directly related to your own company. New ("disruptive") technologies often stimulate new needs, and new opportunities. For example, Amazon.com embraced the concepts of e-books and self-publishers which was a radical departure from print publishers.

Ideas and Actions:

_____

_____

_____

_____

_____

_____

**32. Conduct nominal group technique sessions.** Nominal group technique leverages individual creativity in a group context. In this approach, ask participants to first work alone in silently recording their ideas in writing. Then, collect the written responses and write the responses on a flipchart.

Then, in open discussion, invite additional suggestions based on the charted ideas.

Ideas and Actions:

_____

_____

_____

_____

_____

_____

_____

**33. Identify and focus on higher-level purposes.** Focusing on higher-level purposes for an existing or potential product encourages a broader definition of functions—which can lead to break-through products.

Example: Tape Dispenser

| Component? | • Metal edge that cuts tape |
|---|---|
| Higher-Level Purpose of Component? | • Have the right length of tape for the task at hand |
| Other Ways to Accomplish Same Purpose? | • Sell perforated tape that tears readily (similar to paper towel) without the need for a tape dispenser |

Ideas and Actions:

_____

_____

_____

_____

_____

_____

_____

**34. Develop a product road map.** Outline your vision of the product development process, including exactly when new products will be developed and launched. This encourages designing for the future, in accord with your expectations of market trends.

Example: Sports Equipment New Product Roadmap

Ice Skates & Helmets / 2016 -> Hockey Sticks / 2018 -> Electonic Scoreboards / 2022

Ideas and Actions:

_____

_____

_____

_____

_____

_____

_____

**35. Accentuate the most satisfying characteristics.** Identify what users particularly like about a product—then improve that aspect of it. By this means, you play both to the particular strength of a product and to the expressed preferences of the user.

Example: Automobile Seat

| Characteristic Customers Like Most | Ideas for Accentuating Characteristic |
|---|---|
| • Comfortable seat | • Widen the seat<br>• Provide increased adjustability<br>• Add lumbar support |

Ideas and Actions:

_____

_____

_____

_____

_____

_____

_____

**36. Focus on one criterion at a time.** This technique can be especially effective for products of greater complexity.

Example: Suitcase

| Selection Criteria | Improvement Ideas |
|---|---|
| Ease of rolling | • Larger wheels<br>• More durable wheels<br>• Swiveling wheels |
| Ease of carrying | • Decrease product weight<br>• Add foam to carrying handle<br>• Improve shape, size, or location of handle |
| Storage space | • Increase overall dimensions<br>• Add more case sizes to product line<br>• Make case expandable |

Ideas and Actions:

_____

_____

_____

_____

_____

_____

**37. Allow for incubation.** After (and only after) you have devoted substantial time and effort to a problem, relinquish all creative effort for some interval. Doing so allows your mind to grapple with a problem without conscious effort. It also allows you to reenergize and eventually return to the conscious creative process with a fresh perspective.

Ideas and Actions:

_____

_____

_____

_____

_____

_____

**38. Use a how-to checklist.** Expand the following checklist with additional questions that you find to be good stimulators for brainstorming sessions.

How to make the product last longer?

How to make the product more salable?

How to improve the appearance of the product?

How to improve the packaging?

How to lower the cost?

How to reduce the number of parts?

How to substitute cheaper materials?

How to permit automated assembly?

How to improve safety of the product?

How to improve ease of maintenance and repair?

How to decrease (or increase) the weight of the product?

How to increase performance of the product?

How to decrease (or increase) the operating sound of the product?

How to increase diversity-of-use?

How to increase reliability?

How to improve dimensions of the product?

How to make the product appealing to a rental market?

How to standardize the product, to diversify applicability?

How to make product more susceptible to transport and storage?

How to convert product to digital format?

How to make product recyclable?

How to make product appealing to sharing?

Ideas and Actions:

_____

_____

_____

_____

_____

_____

_____

**39. Apply "analogical reasoning."** Examine areas completely outside of your discipline for inspiration on solutions to problems that may harbor similarities to that of your own.

Example:

"How would a problem such as this be resolved by an animal such as, say—a kangaroo?..."

Ideas and Actions:

_____

_____

_____

_____

_____

_____

_____

**40. Construct matrices comprising market segments and technologies.** In this procedure, the market segments and technologies can be existing, emerging, or future.

Example:

| Technology | Consumer Segment | Commercial Segment |
|---|---|---|
| iPhone | Oil change tracking app | Customer billing app |
| 3D printing | Cup holder attachment app | Engine parts app |

Ideas and Actions:

_____

_____

_____

_____

_____

_____

**41. Construct technology timelines.** Imagine a timeline of emerging technologies. New product ideas and a roadmap for development can then be generated, based on your imagined projections.

Example:  Printer Technology Roadmap

Cloud Programmable / 2016 -> Voice Programmable / 2018 -> Self Programmable / 2022

Ideas and Actions:

_____

_____

_____

_____

———————————————————————

———————————————————————

———————————————————————

**42. Improve attributes, with a focus on competitors.** List attributes of competitors' products; for each attribute, imagine modifications that are superior to those of competing products.

Example: Long-Term Care Medical Bed

| Attribute | Competitors' Product Specs | New Product Specs |
|---|---|---|
| Range of Travel | 21" – 14" | 23" – 12" |
| Supports | Wooden legs | Legs with casters or glide clips |
| Assembly Time | 45 min. (using 22 parts) | 10 min. (using 4 parts) |

Ideas and Actions:

———————————————————————

———————————————————————

———————————————————————

———————————————————————

———————————————————————

———————————————————————

**43. Eliminate biases in idea generation.** Challenge your team to relinquish apparent biases and generate additional ideas not subject to biases. Similarly, challenge your team to generate ideas that fill gaps in generated ideas. For example, if your brainstormed product ideas for calorie counters were all Apple Apps, that would be a bias towards apps. Pushing your team to brainstorm other ideas (e.g., laminated calorie charts, small notebooks) would push them away from their "Apple Apps" bias so a greater variety of solutions was considered.

Ideas and Actions:

_____

_____

_____

_____

_____

_____

**44. Consider product design from the perspective of the business model.** Product designs are often based on particular business models. Imagine products generated by models that diverge from the norm. Example: A service model (recurring charge for services related to the product, rather than the product itself) vs. a disposable product model (one-time charge for a low-cost, disposable product).

Ideas and Actions:

_____

_____

_____

_____

---

---

---

**45. Build prototypes, for customer reviews and product trials**. You can invest different levels of effort in building prototypes. Occasionally, only a prototype to resemble the concept you are proposing is necessary; or you may need more functional prototypes that feel and work very similar to your proposed final product.

Ideas and Actions:

---

---

---

---

---

---

**46. Leverage concept classification trees.** Construct a classification tree whose branches represent product attributes. By identifying various branches, you can ensure you have considered all the possible variations on new product ideas.

Example: Vacuum Cleaners

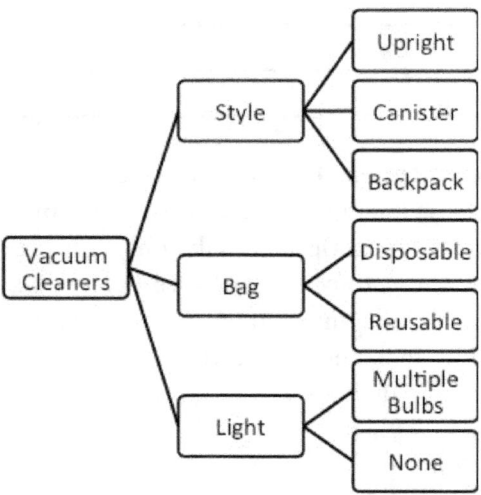

Ideas and Actions:

_____

_____

_____

_____

_____

_____

_____

**47. Construct attribute combination tables.** Tabulate attributes to ensure that all possible combinations are considered.

Example: Vacuum Cleaner

|  | Dry | Wet |
|---|---|---|
| **Upright** | Model A (exists) | Model C (to develop) |
| **Canister** | Model B (to develop) | Model D (exists) |

Ideas and Actions:

_____

_____

_____

_____

_____

_____

_____

**48. De-commoditize a product category.** List products that are commodities in your industry or other industries—that is, products that are differentiated only on the basis of price. Then brainstorm ideas that differentiate new products from existing products on a basis other than price.

Ideas and Actions:

_____

_____

_____

_____

_____

_____

**49. Use "Post-It Notes" to record and organize ideas on the wall.** "Post-It Notes" are a very effective way to maintain momentum in brainstorming sessions. Use such notes to generate, sort, and evaluate ideas. Encourage team members to manipulate the Post-It Notes for fuller engagement in ideation.

Ideas and Actions:

_____

_____

_____

_____

_____

_____

_____

**50. Use outlining software to record and organize ideas.** Outlining software makes it easy to record and shuffle ideas.  For group brainstorming, employ a data projector.

Ideas and Actions:

_____

_____

_____

_____

_____

_____

**51. Keep alternatives alive for as long as possible.** While brainstorming, do not discard unusual ideas too quickly.  During impromptu evaluation, pose "what if...." queries to salvage seemingly impractical possibilities.  Do not discard an idea simply because it does not fit an unusual circumstance. Focus on the more usual conditions, while aiming to adapt ideas to accommodate the unusual.

Ideas and Actions:

_____

_____

_____

_____

_____

_____

**52. Don't imprison yourself with "as-is" data.** Creativity can be hampered if you have become "too expert" on current products. Learn only as much as you need to know about existing products to be familiar with some of their shortcomings—then push yourself to generate creative new product ideas.

Ideas and Actions:

_____

_____

_____

_____

_____

_____

**53. Resist quick resolutions.** After brainstorming, teams sometimes move too quickly to a favorite. This can result in adopting ideas that are simply "safe" or popular. As a result, the chosen idea will probably not be truly innovative. Encourage the team to carefully consider all ideas—especially those that are unusual or not obviously feasible.

Ideas and Actions:

_____

_____

_____

_____

_____

_____

**54. Use mind maps to stimulate divergent thinking.** Mind maps are visual diagrams connecting various topics or concepts related to a common subject. Such maps encourage divergent thinking, or exploration of wholly new topics that may have been initially overlooked. This can lead to new product ideas you had not originally considered.

Example: Starting with the phrase "dog collar"...

Dog Collar → Fur → Fur Coats → Winter → Cold Temps → Wisconsin → Dog collar with University of WI Logo

Ideas and Actions:

_____

_____

_____

_____

_____

_____

**55. Resist the temptation to settle on obvious solutions.** Press yourself for the non-obvious. Playing it safe and generating obvious solutions may be comfortable, yet it all but precludes innovation. Recognize and record the obvious, but always press for the opposite.

Ideas and Actions:

_____

_____

_____

_____

_____

_____

**56. Alternate between solitary work and group work.** Working alone and working as a member of a group each has its own advantages. Some individuals are more comfortable working alone and more likely to generate creative ideas, since evaluation by others is necessarily postponed. But working in a team has the advantage of "piggybacking," which can increase the quantity of ideas. Use both approaches, in alternating bouts.

Ideas and Actions:

_____

_____

_____

_____

_____

**57. Use "I wish...." statements.** Stretch yourself and dream, unabashedly, of ideal products that do not yet exist. Encourage team members to generate new ideas by creating "wish lists."

Ideas and Actions:

_____

_____

_____

_____

_____

_____

**58. Resist over-analysis and perfectionism.** Occasionally, it is better to focus on getting new products to market and fine-tuning later. While launching half-baked products that are certain to fail is never a good ploy, resolving to move quickly and boldly can have its advantages and drive the creativity of your team.

Ideas and Actions:

_____

_____

_____

_____

_____

_____

**59. Sketch your ideas.** Sketches have two advantages: some team members may be visual learners and work more effectively using illustrations; and sketches can help you accelerate development of a concept. Just be careful of artistic perfectionism: even simple stick figures can have significant value.

Ideas and Actions:

_____

_____

_____

_____

_____

_____

**60. Use journey maps.** Journey maps depict the stages through which the customer proceeds before acquiring, and during use of, a product. These may include: research—identification—purchase—use—customization—repair—replacement—discard. Mapping the stages helps you envision ways to optimize the customer experience.

Example: Treadmill Purchase

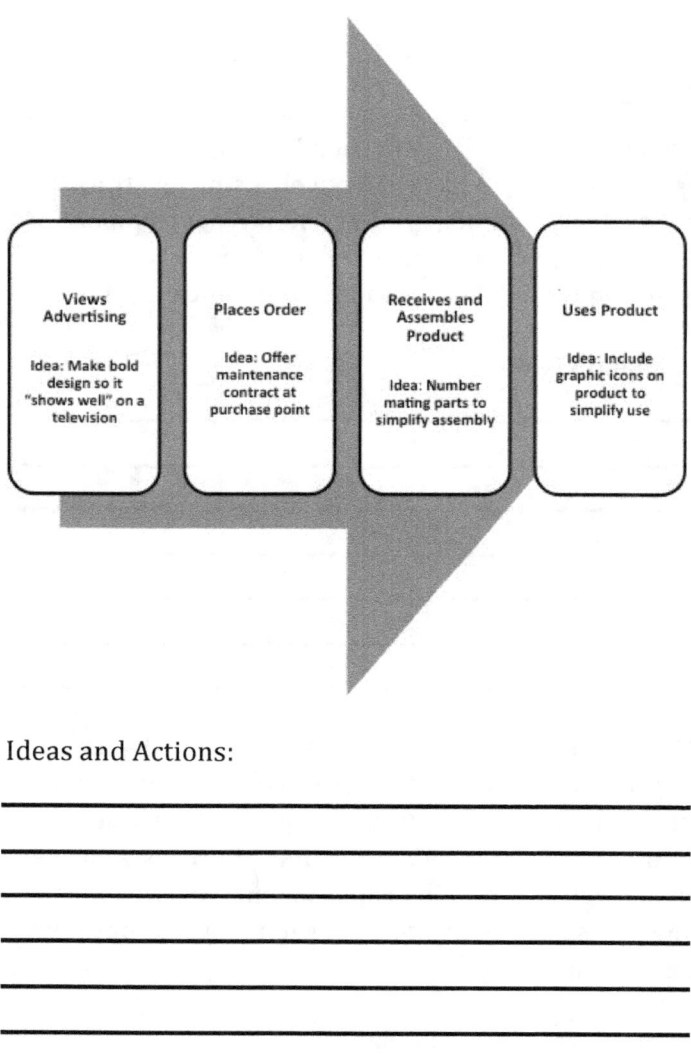

Ideas and Actions:

_____

_____

_____

_____

_____

_____

_____

**61. Break a problem into its parts.** Disassemble larger problems into small components. Establish "milestone" markers so you enjoy a sense of accomplishment as you proceed toward resolution. Intermittent deadlines will lend a sense of urgency in generating ideas, and will tend to diminish the tendency to engage in premature analysis and criticism.

Ideas and Actions:

_____

_____

_____

_____

_____

_____

**62. Apply value analysis techniques.** Identify (or imagine) the major components of a product. For each component, ask whether the component can be eliminated, reduced in cost, improved, combined with another part, and so forth—all with an eye to increasing the overall value of the product.

Example: Wheelchair

| Part | Eliminate? | Combine with Another Part? | Reduce Cost? |
|------|-----------|---------------------------|--------------|
| **224a Hand Grip** | Knurl tube in lieu of separate hand grip | Flare tube into shape of hand grip | Use PVC in lieu of metal |
| **228a Rear Wheel** | (Not feasible) | Combine rear tire and rim | Use PVC in lieu of metal |
| **215a Arm Pad** | Flatten top of tube in lieu of arm piece | Integrate with upper tube | Reduce thickness; use rivets in lieu of screws |

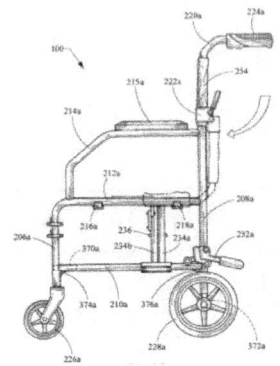

Ideas and Actions:

———————————————————

———————————————————

———————————————————

———————————————————

———————————————————

———————————————————

———————————————————

**63. Apply Maslow's need hierarchy.** The psychologist William Maslow defined a hierarchy of human needs, including: physiological wants (thirst, hunger, sleep); safety (security, protection); love and belonging (friendship, family); esteem (self-esteem, recognition); and self-actualization (psychological growth and development). Try generating product ideas that fulfill the various needs.

Example: Stapler

| Need | Product Idea |
|---|---|
| Physiological | Make top of stapler cushioned so easier on hand |
| Safety | Install guards to protect fingers |
| Love and belonging | N/A |
| Esteem | Create deluxe stapler to offer as a "recognition award" |
| Self-actualization | N/A |

Ideas and Actions:

_____

_____

_____

_____

_____

_____

_____

**64. Leverage a "systems approach" to improving your products.** Identify all your current product's system elements (i.e., inputs, outputs, process & people, metrics, information, financial) and think of new products that are an improvement on each of the elements.

Example: Dishwasher

|  | Inputs | Outputs | Process & People | Metrics | Information | Financial |
|---|---|---|---|---|---|---|
|  | Water Electricity Detergent Dirty dishes | Waste water Clean dishes | Sprays | None | None | Water and energy costs |
| **Product Improvements** | Consume less water and electricity | Reduce waste water by filtering and recirculating | Increase water pressure to clean faster and better | Provide countdown timer showing time remaining | Signal when unit needs servicing | Improve efficiency to cut energy costs |

Ideas and Actions:

_____

_____

_____

_____

_____

_____

**65. Leverage market trends and industry projections.** Consider a broad array of trends including, but not limited to, demographic, social, technological, government trends. Some third-party reports (e.g., Gartner reports) can be purchased to assist with the identification of trends.

Ideas and Actions:

_____

_____

_____

_____

_____

_____

**66. Segment your customers and focus on developing products for each segment.** Be sure to consider new and emerging market segments, which can be a source for innovation in your industry.

Ideas and Actions:

_____

_____

_____

_____

_____

_____

**67. Spend time in foreign countries, identifying needs, and consider developing new products for**

**each country.** This is especially important if you have a strong vision for global distribution.

Ideas and Actions:

_____

_____

_____

_____

_____

_____

_____

**68. Benchmark other companies and industries.** Identify best practices, unsolved problems, and market niche opportunities.

Ideas and Actions:

_____

_____

_____

_____

_____

_____

_____

**69. Drive an innovation "down market."** This involves taking an existing product or technology and figuring out how to make it available to a lower-price point market segment. Crest did this with the Spin Brush. They studied the cordless toothbrush market and discovered that all the cordless toothbrushes seemed to be very expensive. So, they developed a low-cost version of the cordless brush for those who could not afford the higher-priced, feature-rich cordless brushes.

Ideas and Actions:

_____

_____

_____

_____

_____

_____

_____

**70. Identify industries that have not changed in a long time, and brainstorm ideas for new products in these industries.** Slow-changing industries are a good target because customers are usually hungry for new products, and because the market players typically have weak R&D functions, if any at all.

Ideas and Actions:

_____

_____

_____

_____

_____

_____

_____

**71. Identify market threats in an industry and brainstorm creative new products to protect that industry from the market threats.** Threats can include anticipated government regulations, new market entrants, new technologies, and so forth. Anticipating threats and developing new products in advance is a much better strategy than waiting until damage actually occurs and product decisions are being made under duress.

Ideas and Actions:

_____

_____

_____

_____

_____

_____

_____

**72. Develop new products for industries where there are few market players.** When there are only a few market players in an industry, it may indicate little to no change and slow response times. The market may be ripe for a competitive attack.

Ideas and Actions:

_____

_____

_____

_____

_____

_____

_____

**73. Identify and exploit mistakes being made by players in a rapidly-growing industry.** Sometimes, market players in a fast-growing industry are growing so quickly that they are overlooking important, unmet needs. By taking  a step back, and looking for dissatisfied customers or unmet needs, you may spot some potential innovative new product opportunities.

Ideas and Actions:

_____

_____

_____

_____

_____

_____

_____

**74. Identify situations where products are rising in cost due to rising raw material costs.** Brainstorm products that fulfill the same functions but use less expensive materials.

Ideas and Actions:

_____

_____

_____

_____

_____

_____

_____

**75. Identify products on the market that have not been redesigned in a long time.** Brainstorm new product ideas that bring freshness to the market and create high market appeal.

Ideas and Actions:

_____

_____

_____

_____

_____

_____

_____

**76. Identify the role models in a market segment, and brainstorm products that these role models would likely use.** An example would be asking the question, "what type of automobile  would Tiger Woods drive?" Whether you hire the role model later for endorsements is a separate question. But the focus on the role model can help fuel your product development efforts in a great direction.

Ideas and Actions:

_____

_____

_____

_____

_____

_____

_____

**77. Leverage "Porter's Five Forces Framework" in analyzing market dynamics and generating new product ideas.** The five market forces in this framework include: threat of new competitors, bargaining power of suppliers, bargaining power of customers, pressure for substitute products, intensity of rivalry between competitors. Brainstorm new product ideas that overcome or resist these forces in your market.

Ideas and Actions:

_____

_____

_____

_____

_____

_____

**78. Identify your company's competitive advantages and generate new product ideas that leverage these competitive advantages.** Examples of these competitive advantages include: special capabilities, key relationships, brand strengths, geographic advantages, financial access, strategic alliances, low-cost access to key resources, and so forth.

Ideas and Actions:

_____

_____

_____

_____

_____

_____

_____

**79. Leverage competitive comparison matrices to identify your competitors' strengths and weaknesses.** Generate new product ideas that defeat your competitors' strengths and exploit their weaknesses.

Example: Coffee Maker

|  | **Competitor's Strengths** | **Competitor's Weakness** |
|---|---|---|
|  | Low-cost manufacturing source in China | Takes longer to brew a pot of coffee |
| **Product Improvement Ideas for Coffee Maker to Be Superior to Competitor's** | Combine, eliminate, cost reduce coffee maker parts so more competitive | Make coffee maker even faster, and play up the shorter brewing time in all marketing |

Ideas and Actions:

_____

_____

_____

_____

_____

_____

_____

**80. Identify other companies' failed products, and examine root causes.** You may be able to overcome the same mistakes and launch a successful product. Do the same for products that were successful at one time but are no more – asking is there some way to revitalize these once-successful products?

Ideas and Actions:

_____

_____

_____

_____

_____

_____

**81. Identify situations where manufacturers are criticizing their customers – claiming the customers have irrational wants.** Find ways to better satisfy these so-called irrational wants. They may simply be unmet needs waiting to be filled by new, innovative products you create.

Ideas and Actions:

_____

_____

_____

_____

_____

_____

**82. Freshen up existing products with innovative names or color changes.** Do this by coming up with cool names, experimenting with new colors and/or finishes, and spicing up with innovative new features for the same price.

Ideas and Actions:

_____

_____

_____

_____

_____

_____

**83. Focus on leveraging your competitive strategy.** Review what is your competitive strategy (e.g., cost leader, technology leader, customer segment focus, fast imitator). Brainstorm new product ideas that will help you compete even more strongly using your competitive strategy.

Ideas and Actions:

_____

_____

_____

_____

_____

_____

**84. Identify creative new line extensions.** This could include, depending on your product line, additional flavors, additional sizes, additional colors, and so forth.

Ideas and Actions:

_____

_____

_____

_____

_____

_____

**85. Work with lead customers in product development efforts.** Lead customers are those customers who typically are ahead of everyone else in your industry in adopting the latest products, focused on improving their operations, and so forth. Lead customers are typically a rich source for new product ideas and product improvements. In addition to suggesting new products, they are typically very valuable in evaluating your prototypes and being the first to purchase the new products you are launching.

Ideas and Actions:

_____

_____

_____

_____

_____

_____

**86. Identify customer selection criteria and brainstorm on each criterion, one at a time.** Consider rank-ordering the criteria, based on the degree to which they drive the purchasing decision.

Ideas and Actions:

_____

_____

_____

_____

_____

_____

**87. Review customer feedback forms and complaints data.** These can be a rich source of information for companies, but you need to make your customers aware that you actually review and seriously consider the improvement suggestions made. If you do not make them aware, some customers will feel it is a black hole and not bother submitting feedback.

Ideas and Actions:

_____

_____

_____

_____

_____

_____

**88. Leverage the "ethnographic technique" by spending a lot of time observing customers who are using or misusing products.** Ask not only the customers who are directly using your products, but also people related to the actual users (called "unexpected experts"). Act like a beginner and ask very basic, probing, open-ended questions about how they use the product, what they like or do not like, problems they run into, how they are feeling as they use the products, and so forth. Study not only the customers for your products, but also the customers who use your competitors' products. Make audio and video recordings so you can study things more closely later on. As you review the results of your observations, look for patterns and themes, and draw conclusions.

Ideas and Actions:

_____

_____

_____

_____

_____

_____

_____

**89. Form a customer advisory board.** This is an ongoing collection of customers whom you draw upon for brainstorming lists of problems, list of new product ideas, and who review new products you are developing.

Ideas and Actions:

_____

_____

_____

_____

_____

_____

_____

**90. Form an on-line community of enthusiasts who use your product, and monitor their discussions for ideas.** Users will typically share very honest feelings (both positive and negative) about products when talking with other users. You can also seed these conversations by posing as customers and asking questions of other customers.

Ideas and Actions:

_____

_____

_____

_____

_____

_____

**91. Build a "purpose hierarchy" and choose a level on which to focus R&D.** Rephrase customer problem statements into purpose statements, then prioritize these purpose statements, and brainstorm ideas to fulfill the purposes. You can also build "purpose hierarchies" which allow you to more broadly define purposes, opening up a larger opportunity to develop innovative products.

Example: Garden Hose Reel

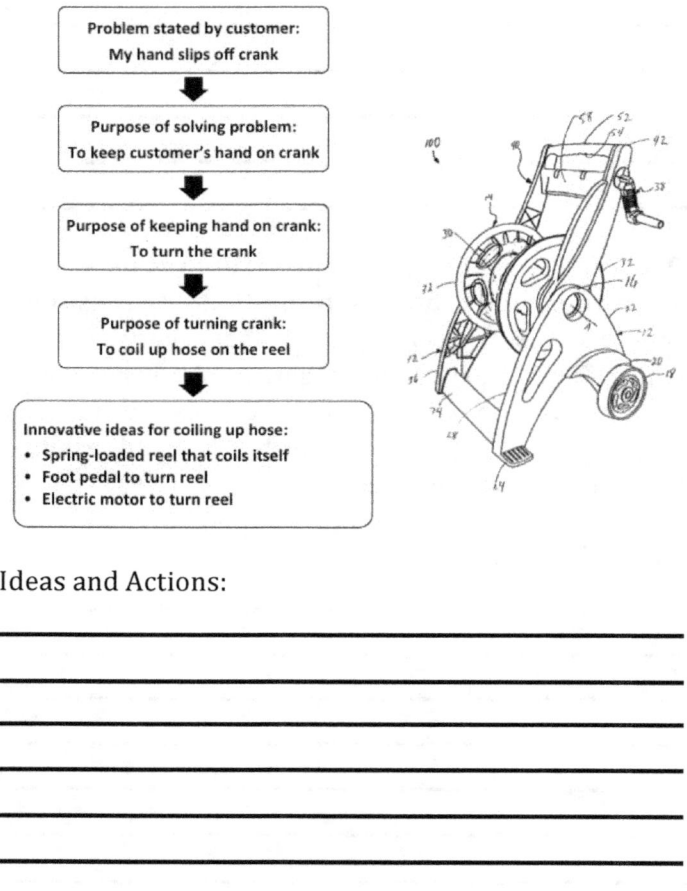

Ideas and Actions:

_____

_____

_____

_____

_____

_____

_____

**92. Carefully understand all the customer touch points with your brand.** Focus on creating the ideal customer experience across all touch points.

Example: Miter Saw for Cutting Wood

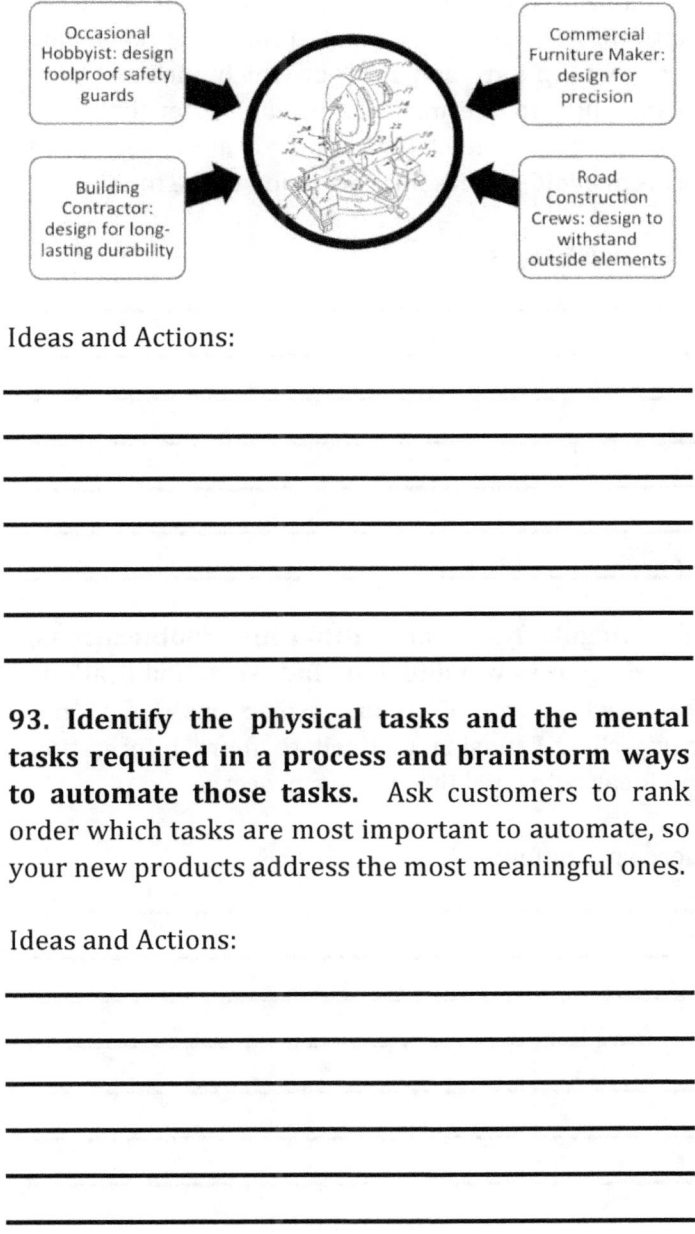

Occasional Hobbyist: design foolproof safety guards

Commercial Furniture Maker: design for precision

Building Contractor: design for long-lasting durability

Road Construction Crews: design to withstand outside elements

Ideas and Actions:

_____

_____

_____

_____

_____

_____

_____

**93. Identify the physical tasks and the mental tasks required in a process and brainstorm ways to automate those tasks.** Ask customers to rank order which tasks are most important to automate, so your new products address the most meaningful ones.

Ideas and Actions:

_____

_____

_____

_____

_____

_____

**94. Challenge assumptions you make about your customers.** Involve your customers in exploring these assumptions, and sort out which ones are most meaningful in terms of product development. Leveraging an outside facilitator can be helpful in terms of avoiding bias interpretation of the findings.

Ideas and Actions:

_____

_____

_____

_____

_____

_____

_____

**95. Regularly read different publications, including ones outside your industry.** Publications are a rich source of trends, projections, ideas, and approaches. Exposing yourself to more information and ideas helps fuel the creative process.

Ideas and Actions:

_____

_____

_____

_____

_____

_____

**96. Review design awards for ideas.** There are both domestic and international product design awards given each year in many industries. Spend time on the Internet looking at these types of awards to find ideas and to gain a better appreciation for the patterns driving the awards.

Ideas and Actions:

_____

_____

_____

_____

_____

_____

**97. Invite independent inventors to submit ideas to your company.** This can be done in several ways. You can contact inventors organizations and tell them what you are looking for. You can also have a section of your web site devoted to inviting product idea submissions. Be sure you provide access to a nondisclosure agreement, so inventors feel protected and more comfortable submitting ideas to your company.

Ideas and Actions:

_____

_____

_____

_____

_____

_____

**98. Review existing and expired patents for ideas.** In some cases you may be able to put a variation on an expired patent and apply for a new patent. In other cases, you may gain a better appreciation for the kinds of problems and approaches an active patent is protecting – leading you to explore alternate approaches and come up with new product ideas. Finally, you may discover "white spaces" which are areas where people have not yet invented or patented products.

Ideas and Actions:

_____

_____

_____

_____

_____

_____

**99. Approach government and university laboratories for technologies they are looking to commercialize.** This source of ideas is typically underutilized by companies. A large proportion of government and university research never results in commercialization in the private sector because of a lack of funding, lack of know-how, or some other reason.

Ideas and Actions:

_____

_____

_____

---

---

---

---

**100. Attend conferences and trade shows.** There are multiple benefits to attending conferences and immersing yourself in a plethora of ideas, establishing contacts with potential suppliers and distributors, talking with customers, hearing from experts, and learning the latest state-of-the art techniques.

Ideas and Actions:

---

---

---

---

---

---

**CHAPTER 5**

# Proceeding to Next Steps

Now that you have read through the Best 100 Strategies, you are undoubtedly very excited to start creating innovative new products. But which of the 100 strategies should you try first? My suggestion is that you take another lap through all the strategies and pick out the top 10 strategies *you* think are the most promising. Then, rank those 10 strategies. It is usually best if you first implement strategies that relate to Involving the Right People and Creating the Right Environment. These two categories of strategies establish more of a "foundation" on which the right processes can be run. If you do not have the right people involved and a creative environment, process improvements will be much less effective. Once you have implemented your top 10 strategies, pick another 10 strategies, and keep implementing more strategies until you have a good flow of innovative, new products coming out of your development pipeline.

Good luck with your new product development efforts!

Top 10 Ideas and Actions from Entire Book:

1 _____

2 _____

3 _____

4 _____

5 _____

6 _____

7 _____

8 _____

9 _____

10 _____

# Recommended Books

Robert G. Cooper, *Winning at New Products: Creating Value Through Innovation* (New York: Basic Books, 2011).

Carmine Gallo, *The Innovation Secrets of Steve Jobs* (New York: McGraw-Hill, 2011).

Tom Kelley and Jonathan Littman, *The Art of Innovation: Lessons in Creativity from IDEO* (New York: Doubleday, 2001).

Tom Kelley and David Kelley, *Creative Confidence: Unleashing the Creative Potential Within Us All* (New York: Crown Publishing Group, 2013).

Gerald Nadler and Shozo Hibino, *Breakthrough Thinking: Why We Must Change the Way We Solve Problems, and the Seven Principles to Achieve This* (Roseville: Prima Publishing, 1989).

Michael Ray and Rochelle Myers, *Creativity in Business* (New York: Broadway Books, 1989).

Karl T. Ulrich, *Product Design and Development* (New York: McGraw-Hill, 2012).

Glen L. Urban and John R. Hauser, *Design and Marketing of New Products* (Englewood-Cliffs: Prentice-Hall, 1993).

Stefanos Zenios, Josh Makower, Paul Yock, Todd J. Brinton, *Biodesign: The Process of Innovating Medical Technologies* (Cambridge: Cambridge University Press, 2010).

# About the Author

Rich Derks is Managing Partner of Innovation360, headquartered in the Chicago area. Innovation360 provides innovation training and full-service new product development for organizations. Over his 25-year career, Derks has developed and launched hundreds of new products for the consumer, medical, and industrial markets. Before starting Innovation360, Derks was president of Medline's Durable Medical Equipment Division, where he had global responsibility for all new product development, manufacturing, and marketing for a wide variety of medical equipment. Derks holds a MBA-Marketing and a BS-Industrial & Systems Engineering, both from the University of Wisconsin-Madison. He is also CPIM certified through APICS. Derks holds multiple patents, and is a frequent speaker at national conferences, Stanford University, MIT, Northwestern, and the University of Wisconsin. He is also an adjunct faculty member with the Illinois Institute of Technology where he teaches a class on business innovation. Rich has published numerous articles on creativity and innovation, and is a past columnist for *Product and Process Innovation*.

www.ingramcontent.com/pod-product-compliance
Lightning Source LLC
Chambersburg PA
CBHW070846180526
45168CB00002B/968